FMCG BLUEPRINT

Your No-Nonsense Guide to FMCG Success!

A No-Nonsense, Real-World Guide to Thriving in FMCG

SURAJ RAINA

ACKNOWLEDGEMENTS

Writing this book has been an exhilarating journey—one filled with endless brainstorming sessions, gallons of coffee, and a newfound appreciation for the magic that happens behind the shelves of every grocery store. **FMCG is not just about products; it's about people.** And this book wouldn't have been possible without a few incredible ones.

First and foremost, **a huge thank you to my mentors, colleagues, and fellow warriors in the FMCG industry**—the ones who shared their insights, challenged my thinking, and made sure I never took the easy route. Your wisdom and experiences have shaped much of what's written in these pages.

To my friends and family—thank you for putting up with my endless rants about supply chains, distributor margins, and why shelf placement is basically a battle for survival. Your patience and encouragement mean the world to me.

A big shoutout to all the **sales reps, merchandisers, distributors, and retail heroes** who make FMCG tick. This book is for you—the ones who hustle every day to get products into customers' hands, who negotiate for every inch of shelf space, and who understand that a great product means nothing if it doesn't move.

To my readers—thank you for picking up this book! Whether you're an FMCG newbie, a seasoned professional, or just someone curious about what happens behind the scenes in the world of fast-moving consumer goods, I hope this book helps you level up your game and see FMCG in a whole new light.

Finally, a special thanks to the brands that have shaped our industry—some of your strategies are in this book, and some of your **blunders** have been used as case studies (no hard feelings, right?).

Here's to making every SKU count!

CONTENTS

ABOUT AUTHOR

Suraj Raina is a sales professional with extensive experience in the FMCG industry, having worked with some of the leading consumer goods companies. A management graduate from SIBM with a specialization in Sales & Marketing, he has spent years navigating the dynamic world of distribution, retail execution, pricing strategies, and brand-building.

With a deep understanding of trade dynamics, consumer psychology, and go-to-market strategies, Suraj has helped brands expand their market presence and drive sales growth. He believes that great execution beats great ideas and that the real battle in FMCG happens at the shelf.

A strong advocate of practical learning over theory, Suraj shares his industry insights, experiences, and no-nonsense sales wisdom in FMCG Blueprint—a book designed to help professionals at all levels thrive in this fast-paced sector.

FOREWORD

The FMCG industry is like a high-stakes reality show—where brands battle for attention, shelf space, and the ultimate prize: **customer loyalty.** It's fast, it's ruthless, and it rewards those who **hustle smart.** If you're in this industry—whether as a sales warrior, marketing ninja, distributor mastermind, or brand builder—you already know that **selling fast-moving consumer goods is a mix of strategy, execution, and a whole lot of caffeine.**

I have spent years in the FMCG trenches, watching brands **rise, fall, and attempt bizarre flavours that nobody asked for (wasabi-flavoured toothpaste, anyone?).** One thing I've learned? **This industry does NOT reward laziness.** The rules keep changing—new channels pop up, consumer tastes shift faster than fashion trends, and technology is shaking up everything from distribution to pricing. If you don't **adapt and outthink the competition,** you might as well start stocking up on "clearance sale" stickers.

This book, **FMCG Blueprint: Your No-Nonsense Guide to FMCG Success,** isn't a sleep-inducing textbook loaded with jargon. **It's a real-world survival guide,** packed with insider insights, strategies, and war stories from the field. Think of it as your **personal cheat code** to navigating and thriving in the FMCG jungle.

Whether you're just getting your feet wet or you've been closing deals longer than some brands have existed, this book will help you:

☑ **Crack the basics**—RTM strategies, channel conflicts, and pricing mysteries solved!

☑ **Master the retail game**—drive availability, visibility, and retailer relationships like a pro.

☑ **Unravel pricing & profitability**—margin, markup, trade promotions? We got you covered.

☑ **Scale like a boss**—from local champ to national or even global powerhouse.

☑ **Prepare for the future**—AI, e-commerce, and sustainability are changing the game, and you need to be ahead.

FMCG isn't just business; **it's a battlefield**, and the winners are those who innovate, execute, and stay two steps ahead.

So, grab your notepad, pour yourself a strong cup of coffee, and get ready to **conquer the world of FMCG**—one SKU at a time.

PART 1:
THE FMCG BASICS –
UNDERSTANDING THE GAME

CHAPTER 1

WHAT THE HELL IS FMCG?
(AND WHY SHOULD YOU CARE?)

Welcome to the world of **Fast-Moving Consumer Goods (FMCG)**—an industry so deeply embedded in your life that you interact with it from the moment you brush your teeth in the morning to the midnight snack raid you pretend never happened. If you've ever bought a shampoo, a pack of biscuits, or a can of soda, congratulations—you've personally contributed to this trillion-dollar industry.

1.1 - FMCG IN A NUTSHELL (OR A PACKET OF CHIPS)

FMCG stands for **Fast-Moving Consumer Goods**, a fancy way of saying "stuff that sells quickly and gets used up just as fast." Think:

- The **toothpaste** you squeeze aggressively when you're running late.
- The **instant noodles** you cook when you're too lazy to make real food.
- The **soft drink** you grab when "just water" feels too healthy.

WHAT MAKES THESE PRODUCTS FMCG?

- ✅ **High turnover** – They move off shelves faster than your boss ignores emails on a Friday evening.
- ✅ **Low cost per unit** – You don't have to sell a kidney to buy them.
- ✅ **Daily/regular consumption** – These aren't luxury yachts; they're everyday essentials.

The global FMCG industry is valued at over **$8 trillion** (Statista, 2023). That's bigger than the GDP of most countries, proving that consumers will never stop buying **soap, snacks, and sodas.**

The FMCG ecosystem is a well-oiled machine with multiple players, each trying to **outsmart, outprice, and outmaneuver** the competition. Let's meet the key stakeholders:

MANUFACTURERS

These are the companies that actually produce your favorite products. Think of giants that invest heavily in **R&D, branding, and packaging** to ensure you **keep choosing their brand over the competition.**

DISTRIBUTORS & WHOLESALERS

These folks ensure FMCG products don't just sit in warehouses but reach millions of retail outlets across the world. They operate massive networks and navigate supply chains that are **more complex than your family WhatsApp group politics.**

RETAILERS

Your local **kirana store, supermarket, hypermarket, or online platform (e-commerce, quick commerce)** is where the magic happens. Retailers are the final step in the FMCG journey, ensuring the products you love (or need) are **just a shelf or a click away.**

CONSUMERS (YES, THAT'S YOU)

Let's be honest—FMCG companies **own your habits.** You may think you "choose" your products, but their marketing teams are two steps ahead, ensuring you can't resist that **buy-one-get-one-free deal** on chips.

What makes FMCG such a money-printing machine? **Three simple reasons:**

1. **Essentials never go out of demand** – Recession, pandemic, war—people still need food, soap, and household goods.
2. **It's all about volume** – Margins are slim, but when you sell in millions, even pennies add up.
3. **Brand loyalty is gold** – If you use a product consistently, there's a good chance you'll keep buying it (unless your dentist intervenes).

💡 **Fun Fact:** Some of the biggest FMCG brands sell over **a billion products daily**, making them an unavoidable part of consumer life.

1.4 - REAL-WORLD FMCG SCENARIOS: THE GOOD, THE BAD & THE UGLY

THE GOOD: THE MAGIC OF DISTRIBUTION

Ever wondered how your favorite chips are available **literally everywhere?** That's **distribution mastery**. A strong distribution network means a product reaches from a rural village store to an urban hypermarket **without missing a beat.**

THE BAD: THE RACE FOR SHELF SPACE

Retail shelves are **prime real estate**. If your product isn't at eye level, it might as well be invisible. Brands **pay** retailers to secure better shelf positioning—a practice called **slotting fees**. And yes, the more you pay, the closer you get to eye level (and impulse buys!).

THE UGLY: WHEN A BRAND FLOPS

Not every FMCG launch is a success. Sometimes, even industry giants misjudge consumer preferences, proving that **FMCG is as much about psychology** as it is about sales.

FMCG is evolving faster than ever. The rise of **D2C (Direct-to-Consumer) brands, e-commerce, AI-driven personalization, and sustainability-focused innovations** is changing how brands operate. The next decade will see:

- ☑ **More AI-driven sales & marketing strategies**
- ☑ **A stronger push towards sustainability & eco-friendly packaging**
- ☑ **A major shift towards digital commerce and online brand engagement**

1.6 - CLOSING THOUGHTS: WHY THIS BOOK WILL MAKE YOU AN FMCG NINJA

FMCG isn't just about products—it's about **strategy, execution, and understanding what makes consumers tick**. This book will take you from **FMCG newbie to industry pro,** equipping you with insights, real-world case studies, and strategies used by the biggest brands.

 **COMING UP NEXT**

The FMCG Battlefield – Who's Fighting for Your Money?

(Hint: It's a war you never noticed, but you're already a part of it.)

CHAPTER 2
THE FMCG BATTLEFIELD – WHO'S FIGHTING FOR YOUR MONEY?

Welcome to the warzone. You might not see tanks and soldiers, but make no mistake - FMCG is a **battlefield** where brands, retailers, and distributors engage in **a never-ending war** for shelf space, market share, and, ultimately, your money. Every time you pick up a bottle of cola or a pack of chips, you're casting a vote in a competition fiercer than any reality show.

2.1 - THE THREE GIANTS OF FMCG: WHO RUNS THE SHOW?

The FMCG battlefield has three major power players:

1. MANUFACTURERS: THE POWERHOUSES

These are the big brands that **create and market products**. Companies like **Nestlé, Unilever, Procter & Gamble, and ITC** spend billions on **product innovation, aggressive marketing, and cutting-edge supply chains.**

Case Study: Coca-Cola vs. RC Cola – The Power of Distribution

Ever wondered why Coca-Cola dominates every store while RC Cola struggles for space? It's not just brand love—**it's distribution power.**

☑ Coca-Cola has invested in deep rural penetration, ensuring availability even in remote villages.

☑ RC Cola, despite being a good product, fails because it lacks strong distributor partnerships.

☑ Coca-Cola provides higher retailer incentives, ensuring prime placement at cash counters.

👉 **Lesson:** The best product doesn't always win—**the best-distributed product does.**

2. DISTRIBUTORS & WHOLESALERS: THE HIDDEN MIDDLEMEN

Distributors act as **the link between manufacturers and retailers.** They **buy in bulk, manage logistics, and ensure product availability.**

Case Study: The Energy Drink That Died Before It Lived

A premium energy drink launched in **India's metro cities** with huge digital campaigns. But within **six months, the brand vanished.** Why?

✖ **Distributors were reluctant to stock an unknown brand.**

✖ **Retailers demanded high margins, making the drink too expensive.**

❌ **Stock-outs killed momentum—customers didn't find it twice, so they moved on.**

👉 **Lesson:** Without strong distribution, even a viral brand can die fast.

3. RETAILERS: THE GATEKEEPERS OF SALES

Retailers **control visibility and final purchase decisions.** They decide which products get premium shelf space and which ones get **hidden in the corner.**

Example: The Mystery of Eye-Level Shelf Space

Have you noticed why some brands **always** appear at eye level in supermarkets while others are placed at the bottom? That's called **slotting fees.**

✅ **Big brands PAY supermarkets to place their products where shoppers naturally look first.**

✅ **Retailers prioritize brands that offer the best margins, discounts, and trade schemes.**

✅ **New brands often struggle because they cannot afford high slotting fees.**

👉 **Lesson:** The battle is not just in ads—it's fought on supermarket shelves.

2.2 - THE RETAIL WAR:
GENERAL TRADE (GT) VS. MODERN TRADE (MT) VS. E-COMMERCE

1. GENERAL TRADE (GT): THE LOCAL CHAMPIONS

Think **kirana stores, paan shops, small grocery stores.** These are still **70%** of India's FMCG market.

 Example: Maggi's rural success isn't just about brand love. It's because **Nestlé ensures Maggi is stocked in every kirana store, even in villages with no supermarkets.**

☑ **Strengths:** High trust, immediate access, local influence.

✕ **Weaknesses:** Cash transactions, limited shelf space.

2. MODERN TRADE (MT): THE ORGANIZED RETAILERS

Big supermarket chains like **D-Mart, Big Bazaar, and Reliance Fresh.**

 Example: Why does D-Mart sell household essentials at the lowest price? **Because it buys in bulk from manufacturers at a discount.**

☑ **Strengths:** Bulk sales, data tracking, impulse purchases.

✕ **Weaknesses:** High listing fees, delayed payments.

3. E-COMMERCE: THE DIGITAL DISRUPTORS

Amazon, Blinkit, Zepto, and Flipkart are **changing FMCG with fast delivery and deep discounts.**

Case Study: The ₹1 Durex Condom Offer on Amazon

 Durex India once ran a **₹1 condom offer on Amazon.** Within **hours, the listing had thousands of purchases.**

☑ Why?

- o   Digital platforms allow extreme price flexibility.

- o   Offers go viral due to instant social media exposure.
- o   Direct-to-consumer (D2C) eliminates retailer dependency.

❌ **Risk?** Such discounts **anger general trade retailers**, leading them to boycott the brand.

👉 **Lesson:** Digital sales are the future, but brands must balance online and offline relationships.

2.3 - CHANNEL CONFLICT: WHEN GT, MT, AND E-COMMERCE FIGHT EACH OTHER

Ever noticed the **same product priced differently in supermarkets vs. local shops vs. online?** That's channel conflict.

Example: The Shampoo Price War

A new **shampoo brand launched at ₹100 in supermarkets.** But Flipkart and Amazon started selling it for **₹85** due to promotional discounts.

Result? Kirana shop owners got angry, stopped stocking the product.

Fix? The brand introduced **different pack sizes**—250ml for supermarkets, 200ml for local stores, and combo packs for e-commerce.

Lesson: Avoid direct price wars—use unique SKUs for different channels.

2.4 - WINNING STRATEGIES: TRADE MARKETING & IN-STORE EXECUTION

Trade marketing helps brands **own shelf space, influence last-mile sales, and ensure better product visibility.**

- ✅ **Planogram Mastery:** Products must be at **eye level** for maximum sales.
- ✅ **Retailer Incentives:** Give higher margins to retailers who stock more.
- ✅ **POS Material Dominance:** Bright display stands, danglers, shelf talkers.
- ✅ **Mystery Shopping:** Send auditors to check if stores **are displaying your brand correctly.**

Case Study:
Why Pepsi Paid Retailers to Stock Mountain Dew in Summer

During peak summer, retailers naturally stock **Coca-Cola over Pepsi.** So what did Pepsi do?

🚀 They **PAID kirana store owners ₹500 extra** per month to stock **Mountain Dew near their cash counters.**

This led to a **15% increase in impulse purchases.**

👉 **Lesson:** If you can't beat the competition, **out-incentivize them.**

2.5 - FINAL THOUGHTS: FMCG IS WAR—PICK YOUR BATTLES WISELY

FMCG is a warzone where brands **fight for shelf space, visibility, and pricing control.** The **winners are those who:**

- ☑ **Control distribution better than competitors.**
- ☑ **Optimize pricing across GT, MT, and E-commerce.**
- ☑ **Execute in-store strategies flawlessly.**

Route-to-Market (RTM) – The Art of Getting Products Everywhere
(Hint: Even the best product is useless if it doesn't reach the right shelf at the right time).

PART 2:
CRACKING
THE FMCG SALES CODE

CHAPTER 3
ROUTE-TO-MARKET (RTM) –
THE ART OF GETTING PRODUCTS EVERYWHERE

Welcome to the beating heart of FMCG success: **Route-to-Market (RTM)**. You can have the best product in the world, but if it doesn't reach the right shelf at the right time, it might as well not exist. RTM is what separates the **winners** from the "oh, we had a great product, but no one bought it" crowd.

The FMCG business is defined by **speed, availability, and affordability.** Even the strongest brands can lose customers if they don't ensure the **right product, in the right place, at the right time, at the right price.**

KEY REASONS WHY RTM IS CRITICAL:

- ✅ **Ensures Product Availability** – If the product isn't available at the point of purchase, there's **zero** chance of a sale. RTM ensures your product reaches **every intended store and platform.**

- ✅ **Reduces Cost-to-Serve** – The **wrong RTM strategy can eat into profits.** Optimized RTM ensures minimum logistics and warehousing costs.

- ✅ **Enhances Competitive Advantage** – A well-structured RTM creates a **wider distribution footprint, stronger retailer relationships, and faster replenishment cycles.**

- ✅ **Supports Market Expansion** – The choice of RTM **determines how quickly** a brand can scale into **new cities, towns, and rural markets.**

- ✅ **Improves Trade Relationships** – A well-executed RTM **builds trust with distributors, wholesalers, and retailers**, ensuring smoother operations.

📌 CASE STUDY: HOW MAGGI BOUNCED BACK AFTER A NATIONWIDE BAN

In **2015, Maggi was banned in India** due to safety concerns, leading to a **complete market exit.** Once it cleared regulatory approvals, **Nestlé had to rebuild its entire distribution network from scratch.**

How they did it:

- Used their **deep distributor relationships** to **relist Maggi in every kirana store and supermarket.**

- **Launched aggressive marketing campaigns** with the message: *"Your favorite noodles are back!"*

- **Ensured high availability** in rural and urban centers simultaneously.

🚀 **Within 6 months, Maggi regained 70% of its lost market share!**

👉 **Lesson:** RTM isn't just about sales—it's about resilience, recovery, and long-term availability.

3.2 - KEY RTM MODELS & THEIR COMPLEXITIES

FMCG brands use **multiple RTM models** based on **product type, market maturity, operational costs, and consumer demand.**

Let's break down the most important RTM strategies used in FMCG:

1. DIRECT DISTRIBUTION – WHEN SPEED IS KING

🚀 Best for **perishable goods, dairy, bakery, beverages, and fresh produce**

How it Works:

- The company **directly delivers** products to retailers without intermediaries.

- Requires **high logistical investment** but ensures **freshness, better control, and faster replenishment cycles.**

- Common in **dairy, bakery, fresh vegetables, and beverage businesses.**

Complexities:

❌ **Requires a strong fleet** (trucks, delivery vans, cold chains for dairy, frozen products, and beverages).

❌ **High operational costs** due to logistics and last-mile delivery.

❌ **Challenging in geographically dispersed markets.**

📌 **Example: Amul's Direct Distribution Model**

Amul follows a direct distribution model to ensure its milk and dairy products are always **fresh and available daily.**

👉 **Lesson:** Direct distribution is **high cost but essential for fresh product categories.**

2. DISTRIBUTOR-BASED MODEL – THE MOST COMMON RTM

🛒 Best for **packaged foods, snacks, beverages, and household products**

How it Works:

- o The company sells products to **distributors**, who then supply thousands of retailers.
- o Ideal for **mass-market FMCG products with frequent demand cycles.**

Complexities:

✖ **Brands have lower control over in-store execution and retailer relationships.**

✖ **Distributors often push competing brands that offer higher margins.**

✖ **Stockouts can occur if distributors fail to restock on time.**

📌 **Example: Parle-G's Mass Distribution Success** Parle-G's biscuits reach even the most remote villages **because of their massive distributor network.**

👉 **Lesson:** Distributors **allow scale but reduce brand control.**

3. WHOLESALE MODEL – BULK SELLING FOR HIGH-VOLUME PRODUCTS

🏪 Best for **low-margin, high-rotation products (detergents, staples, toiletries)**

How it Works:

- o The company sells products to **wholesalers**, who then distribute to thousands of retailers.
- o Used when **distributor margins are too high** or in **price-sensitive rural markets.**

Complexities:

✖ **Wholesalers can hoard stock, creating artificial supply shortages.**

✖ **Poor brand control over product visibility in stores.**

📌 **Example: Patanjali's Wholesale Expansion Strategy** Patanjali products spread nationwide through **wholesale-led distribution, ensuring availability across all rural markets.**

👉 **Lesson:** Wholesale provides **wide reach but minimal control.**

📌 **Problem:** Modern trade, e-commerce, and general trade **often compete against each other**, leading to pricing conflicts and retailer dissatisfaction.

🪨 Example: The ₹100 Shampoo Pricing Conflict

- o A leading shampoo brand launched at ₹100 in **supermarkets.**
- o Flipkart and Amazon **started selling it for ₹85**, using discounts.
- o Kirana store owners **felt cheated and stopped stocking it.**

✅ **Solution:** Brands create **differentiated SKUs** (pack sizes) to avoid direct comparisons.

👉 **Lesson: Channel harmony is critical to avoid retailer pushback.**

The best brands **don't just market better—they distribute smarter.**

- ✅ **Choose the right RTM mix based on product type.**
- ✅ **Use AI and data to prevent stockouts.**
- ✅ **Optimize supply chain costs for higher profitability.**

The Science of Sales – How to Move Products Like a Pro!

CHAPTER 4

THE SCIENCE OF SALES – HOW TO MOVE PRODUCTS LIKE A PRO

Sales in FMCG isn't about charm and a firm handshake anymore. It's a **highly structured, data-driven, and execution-focused** discipline where the right strategy can skyrocket revenues while a small mistake can bury even the best products. The battle isn't just about selling—it's about **who sells smarter**.

4.1 - THE THREE PILLARS OF FMCG SALES SUCCESS

Winning in FMCG sales boils down to three fundamental pillars:

1. AVAILABILITY – ENSURING YOUR PRODUCT IS ALWAYS PRESENT

No matter how great your product is, **if it's not available on the shelf, it cannot sell.** Ensuring **high product availability across all sales channels** is the foundation of FMCG success.

How to Maximize Availability:

- ☑ **Distributor Stock Planning:** Maintain optimal stock levels at distributor warehouses to avoid stockouts.
- ☑ **Retailer Replenishment Cycles:** Understand the frequency at which retailers place orders and ensure they never run out.
- ☑ **Perfect Store Execution:** Conduct audits to check if your product is actually stocked at outlets.

➤ **Case Study: How Coca-Cola Ensures 100% Availability** Coca-Cola's success is built on **one simple principle: You should never have to search for a Coke.** Their distribution model ensures availability **in every kirana store, supermarket, and vending machine.**

👉 **Lesson:** The best products don't win by just being good—they win by being **always available.**

2. VISIBILITY – WINNING THE RETAIL SHELF SPACE BATTLE

FMCG sales is not just about having a product in the store—it's about **where** the product is placed.

Why Visibility Matters:

- **Eye-Level = Buy-Level** – Products placed at **eye level** sell 30-50% more than those placed at the bottom shelf.
- **Branded POSM (Point of Sale Materials)** – Shelf talkers, posters, danglers, and in-store branding **increase product recall.**

- **End-Cap Displays & Cash Counter Placement** – Products at checkout counters and **end-of-aisle displays** get higher impulse purchases.

🔹 **Example: How Lays Dominates Supermarkets** Lays ensures **maximum visibility** by occupying premium shelf space, placing large branded racks at store entrances, and using **limited-time offers to capture consumer attention.**

👉 **Lesson:** If your product is not **seen**, it will not be **picked up.**

3. RETAILER RELATIONSHIPS – THE KEY TO LONG-TERM SUCCESS

Retailers play a **critical role** in deciding which products they actively promote. The stronger your relationship with retailers, **the more they push your brand.**

How to Strengthen Retailer Relationships:

✅ **Retailer Incentives:** Offer better margins, discounts, and trade promotions to retailers who actively promote your product.

✅ **Trust & Consistency:** Ensure timely deliveries and avoid stock shortages.

✅ **Exclusive Deals:** Give first access to new products to your best-performing retailers.

🔹 **Example: How ITC Gained Retailer Loyalty for Aashirvaad Atta** ITC offered **higher trade margins, quicker restocking cycles, and exclusive deals** to retailers who pushed Aashirvaad Atta over competing brands.

👉 **Lesson:** Treat your retailers as partners, not just sales points.

Understanding how consumers make decisions **inside the store** is key to increasing sales. The FMCG buying journey is usually **impulse-driven**, but the right sales tactics can influence decisions.

STAGES OF AN FMCG PURCHASE DECISION:

1. Awareness (Attract Attention)

- **In-store branding, promotions, and sampling** attract first-time buyers.
- **Retail staff influence** plays a major role in traditional trade.

2. Consideration (Shelf Appeal Matters)

- **Price comparison, pack sizes, and perceived value** impact purchase.
- **Packaging innovation (resealable packs, eco-friendly materials) can differentiate products.**

3. Purchase (Final Decision Point)

- **Last-mile triggers like limited-time discounts, BOGO (Buy-One-Get-One) offers, and bundling increase conversion.**

 Example: How Dettol Uses In-Store Sampling to Drive Sales Dettol often places **free hand sanitizer dispensers** in stores, reminding consumers of hygiene before they even reach the aisle.

 Lesson: The **moment of truth** happens at the retail shelf. Influence that, and you win.

4.3 - FIELD SALES VS. KEY ACCOUNT MANAGEMENT – DIFFERENT APPROACHES

FMCG sales teams are **divided into two major functions:**

1. Field Sales (General Trade / Traditional Trade)

- Sales reps visit **kirana stores, small retailers, and distributors** to drive orders.
- Focus on **quick turnarounds, stock checks, and promotional schemes.**
- Example: **Parle sales reps regularly visit local stores to ensure strong availability of Parle-G biscuits.**

2. Key Account Management (Modern Trade & E-Commerce)

- Works with **supermarkets (D-Mart, Big Bazaar) and e-commerce giants (Amazon, Blinkit).**
- Involves **long-term negotiations, annual contracts, and promotional planning.**
- Example: **Nestlé negotiates yearly deals with Walmart to secure premium shelf placements.**

 Lesson: Both field sales and key account management are essential for a **strong sales mix.**

Sales is no longer just about relationships—it's about **data-driven decision-making.** Companies use technology to predict demand, track sales trends, and optimize supply chains.

Key Tech Trends in FMCG Sales:

- **AI & Predictive Analytics:** Helps brands forecast demand spikes (e.g., increased soft drink demand in summer).

- **CRM & Sales Automation:** Ensures real-time stock tracking, reducing stockouts.

- **Retail Analytics & Mystery Shopping:** Audits product placement and retailer compliance.

Case Study: How Pepsi Uses AI for Sales Planning PepsiCo uses **AI-driven sales forecasts** to predict high-demand zones and **adjust distribution accordingly,** ensuring they never run out during peak seasons.

Lesson: Brands that use **data and automation** gain a competitive edge.

The best FMCG sales teams don't just **sell**—they **optimize execution, build trust, and use data to stay ahead.**

- ✅ **Ensure product availability at all times.**
- ✅ **Invest in visibility – eye-level shelf placement wins.**
- ✅ **Retailer relationships can make or break your success.**
- ✅ **Leverage AI and data analytics to improve forecasting.**

The Dark Art of Pricing – Markup, Margin & How Brands Make Money!

PART 3:
THE MONEY GAME –
MARGINS, MARKUPS, AND ROI

CHAPTER 5

THE DARK ART OF PRICING – MARKUP, MARGIN & HOW BRANDS MAKE MONEY

Pricing in FMCG isn't just about slapping a number on a product—it's an **art, a science, and sometimes even a bit of psychological warfare.** Set it too high, and consumers will dump you for the cheaper alternative. Set it too low, and your margins vanish faster than a free sample at a grocery store.

1. MARKUP VS. MARGIN: THE FOUNDATION OF PRICING

☑ **Markup** = The percentage added to the cost price to determine the selling price.

☑ **Margin** = The percentage of revenue that remains after deducting costs.

📌 **Formula:**

Marup = (Selling Price – Cost Price)/Cost Price *100

Margin = (Selling Price – Cost Price)/Selling Price *100

• **Example:** If a biscuit manufacturer produces a pack at ₹10 and sells it to retailers at ₹15:

- o **Markup** = (15-10)/10 * 100 = **50%**
- o **Margin** = (15-10)/15 * 100 = **33.3%**

👉 **Lesson:** High markups do not always mean high margins. Understanding the difference is crucial for setting the right price.

2. COST COMPONENTS THAT INFLUENCE PRICING

A product's price must cover multiple cost layers to be profitable. The key cost components include:

☑ **Raw Material Costs** – Ingredients, packaging materials, and processing.

☑ **Manufacturing & Labor** – Costs associated with production and wages.

☑ **Distribution & Logistics** – Transport, warehousing, and last-mile delivery.

☑ **Retailer Margins** – The cut taken by distributors and retailers.

☑ **Marketing & Trade Promotions** – Discounts, in-store branding, and TV/digital ads.

☑ **Taxes & Regulatory Costs** – GST, import duties, and compliance expenses.

📌 **Example: How Price Composition Works in a ₹100 Shampoo Bottle**

- o ₹30 = Manufacturing & raw materials
- o ₹10 = Distribution & logistics
- o ₹20 = Retailer & distributor margins

o   ₹25 = Marketing & advertising

o   ₹15 = Profit margin

👉 **Lesson:** Pricing is not just about profit—it must **recover costs and still be attractive to consumers.**

Pricing is **not just about numbers—it's about consumer perception.** Brands use psychological tactics to drive purchases.

1. Charm Pricing – The Power of ₹99.99

- Consumers associate ₹99 with 'less than ₹100' even though the difference is ₹1.
- Common in packaged snacks, personal care, and beverages.

2. Price Anchoring – Creating a Perceived Deal

- Displaying an 'original price' with a slashed 'discounted price' makes the deal look more attractive.
- Used heavily in e-commerce, modern trade, and combo offers.

3. Unit Price Manipulation – Playing with Pack Sizes

- Reducing pack size while maintaining price ('shrinkflation').
- Used in chocolates, chips, and biscuits to maintain margins without increasing MRP.

◆ **Example: Why a ₹10 Lay's Packet Feels Empty?** Lay's maintains **the same price** but **reduces net weight per pack** to manage inflation and input cost hikes.

☞ **Lesson:** Smart pricing strategies influence consumer perception and boost sales.

5.3 - DIFFERENT PRICING STRATEGIES USED IN FMCG

1. PENETRATION PRICING – WINNING WITH LOWER PRICES

- Used when entering new markets or launching new products.
- Attracts customers by undercutting competitors.
- Once market share is built, brands gradually increase prices.

📌 **Example: How Colgate Defeated Pepsodent in India** Colgate introduced **₹10 toothbrushes** to **block Pepsodent from gaining traction.**

👉 **Lesson:** Penetration pricing works but requires deep pockets.

2. PREMIUM PRICING – SELLING PERCEIVED VALUE

- Used for high-end or niche products.
- Relies on strong branding, luxury perception, and limited availability.

📌 **Example: Why Dove Shampoos Cost More Than Clinic Plus?** Dove positions itself as a **'moisturizing beauty shampoo'** rather than a basic hair cleaner.

👉 **Lesson:** Premium pricing is about branding, not just the product.

3. ECONOMY PRICING – WINNING AT LOW COST

- Targets price-sensitive customers with 'no-frills' pricing.
- Used by mass-market brands like Big Bazaar's private labels.

📌 **Example: Why D-Mart Sells FMCG Cheaper Than Supermarkets?** D-Mart buys directly from manufacturers in bulk, eliminating **distributor costs.**

👉 **Lesson:** Economy pricing works when operational costs are minimized.

4. DYNAMIC PRICING – PRICE ADJUSTMENTS BASED ON DEMAND

- Used in e-commerce and online grocery platforms.

- AI-based models adjust prices based on demand trends.

Example: How Amazon Changes FMCG Prices Hourly Amazon uses **machine learning** to adjust FMCG prices based on competitor pricing, sales trends, and stock levels.

Lesson: Dynamic pricing is the future of modern retail.

Pricing alone is not enough—**discounts and promotions play a crucial role in sales velocity.**

☑ **Trade Discounts:** Given to distributors for bulk purchases.

☑ **Consumer Promotions:** Buy-one-get-one (BOGO), free samples, and cashback.

☑ **Seasonal Offers:** Higher discounts during festivals or special events.

☑ **Retailer Incentives:** Extra margins to retailers who meet sales targets.

📌 **Example: Why Cadbury Offers Freebies During Diwali** Cadbury increases pack size **without changing MRP** during festive seasons to boost bulk sales.

👉 **Lesson:** Promotions should increase sales without diluting brand value.

- ☑ Margins must be optimized for profitability without hurting consumer affordability.
- ☑ Pricing psychology plays a crucial role in FMCG success.
- ☑ Different pricing strategies work for different categories—choose wisely.
- ☑ Promotions should be designed to increase long-term brand loyalty, not just short-term sales.

ROI Demystified – How to Know if Your FMCG Business is Winning!

CHAPTER 6

ROI DEMYSTIFIED – HOW TO KNOW IF YOUR FMCG BUSINESS IS ACTUALLY WINNING

Return on Investment (**ROI**) is the ultimate reality check for any FMCG business. You might be selling truckloads of products, but if the numbers don't add up, your brand is just a **glorified charity**. Understanding ROI isn't just for finance geeks—it's for **anyone who wants to make sure every rupee spent brings back more.**

Return on Investment (ROI) in FMCG is not just about **profits**—it's about maximizing **efficiency across operations, sales, and marketing.** Unlike premium goods, where **higher margins drive profitability,** FMCG companies must focus on **reducing costs, optimizing supply chains, and increasing volume sales.**

Key Metrics to Track ROI in FMCG:

- ✅ **Gross Margin (%)** – The difference between revenue and the cost of goods sold (COGS).
- ✅ **Net Profit Margin (%)** – The actual profit after deducting all operational expenses.
- ✅ **Stock Turnover Ratio** – How frequently inventory is sold and replaced within a given period.
- ✅ **Trade Spend ROI (%)** – How much revenue is generated per unit spent on trade promotions.
- ✅ **Customer Lifetime Value (CLV)** – The total revenue expected from a single customer over their buying cycle.

📌 **Example: How Nestlé Improved ROI in Dairy Business** Nestlé optimized its dairy supply chain by **reducing milk procurement costs and implementing predictive demand analytics**, increasing its net profit margin from **9% to 12%** within two years.

👉 **Lesson: ROI is not just about sales—it's about profitability across every business function.**

Pricing in FMCG is delicate—**too high, and you lose volume sales; too low, and margins collapse.** Brands must balance **competitive pricing, retailer margins, and customer willingness to pay.**

Types of Pricing Models in FMCG:

☑ **Cost-Plus Pricing** – Adding a fixed markup over production costs. Simple but risky in competitive categories.

☑ **Value-Based Pricing** – Pricing based on perceived customer value rather than cost (e.g., premium organic foods).

☑ **Dynamic Pricing** – Adjusting prices based on real-time demand, competitor pricing, or regional preferences.

☑ **Freemium & Bundling** – Offering free samples, combo packs, or "Buy One, Get One Free" deals to increase uptake.

🔖 **Example: How HUL Adjusted Pricing for Rural Expansion** HUL introduced **₹1 shampoo sachets** to penetrate rural markets, balancing **low margins with high volume sales**, resulting in **30% higher rural penetration.**

👉 **Lesson: Pricing should be a strategic tool, not just a number.**

Efficient inventory management is critical for **reducing wastage, lowering carrying costs, and ensuring timely replenishment.** Poor inventory control can lead to **stockouts (lost sales) or overstocking (dead inventory and higher costs).**

Key Strategies for Inventory Optimization:

- ☑ **Just-in-Time (JIT) Inventory** – Maintaining low stock levels and replenishing frequently to reduce holding costs.

- ☑ **FIFO & LIFO Approaches** – Using First-In-First-Out (FIFO) for perishable goods and Last-In-First-Out (LIFO) for products with fluctuating costs.

- ☑ **Demand Forecasting Using AI** – Predictive analytics to anticipate sales trends and avoid over/understocking.

- ☑ **Vendor Managed Inventory (VMI)** – Outsourcing stock management to suppliers for improved replenishment accuracy.

📌 **Example: How Walmart Cut Supply Chain Costs by 20%** Walmart used **AI-driven demand forecasting** to align supply with customer behavior, reducing stock-outs by **15% and overstock by 10%**, improving overall ROI.

👉 **Lesson: A lean supply chain ensures better cash flow and profitability.**

6.4 - TRADE PROMOTIONS & RETAILER INCENTIVES

Trade promotions consume **15-30% of FMCG marketing budgets**, yet **only some promotions lead to higher sales.** Brands must invest in **high-ROI trade incentives that drive retailer participation and consumer pull.**

Effective Trade Promotion Strategies:

- ☑ **Buy-Back Guarantees** – Encouraging retailers to stock more with risk-free returns.
- ☑ **Volume-Based Incentives** – Offering better margins for retailers who stock larger volumes.
- ☑ **Limited-Time Shelf Space Deals** – Paying retailers for premium positioning (eye-level shelving, checkout counter placements).
- ☑ **Targeted Discounting** – Offering discounts **only in high-elasticity regions** instead of pan-India markdowns.

📌 **Example: How Mondelez Increased Shelf Space for Dairy Milk** Mondelez **offered 15% higher margins to retailers** who stocked Dairy Milk near the checkout counter, increasing impulse sales by **25%.**

👉 **Lesson: Trade promotions should be precise, not just broad discounting.**

6.5 - MARKETING ROI – MAXIMIZING IMPACT WITH LIMITED BUDGETS

Marketing spends must be **carefully measured** to ensure **higher return on ad spend (ROAS)**. Traditional ads, digital marketing, and in-store promotions must **align with consumer buying behavior.**

High-ROI Marketing Tactics in FMCG:

☑ **Hyperlocal Digital Campaigns** – Using targeted Facebook/Google ads to reach consumers near retail stores.

☑ **Influencer Marketing for Niche Categories** – Partnering with micro-influencers instead of spending on celebrity endorsements.

☑ **Retail Activation Programs** – Sampling campaigns inside supermarkets boost trial rates **3x more than traditional ads.**

☑ **Gamification & Loyalty Programs** – Offering points, cashback, or exclusive deals to drive repeat purchases.

📌 **Example: How Red Bull Maximized ROI with Experiential Marketing** Instead of traditional advertising, Red Bull focused on **extreme sports sponsorships and social media buzz,** keeping marketing ROI **70% higher than category competitors.**

👉 **Lesson: Marketing should be performance-driven, not just awareness-based.**

6.6 - CONTROLLING OPERATIONAL COSTS WITHOUT CUTTING GROWTH

FMCG brands must balance **cost-cutting with growth investments.** Many companies make the mistake of cutting **marketing, trade promotions, or R&D**, which hurts long-term scalability.

Key Areas for Cost Optimization:

☑ **Reducing Packaging Costs** – Using eco-friendly, lower-cost packaging materials while maintaining brand aesthetics.

☑ **Outsourcing Non-Core Activities** – Using third-party logistics (3PL) for distribution instead of in-house fleets.

☑ **Energy Efficiency in Manufacturing** – Using automation and renewable energy to lower factory costs.

☑ **SKU Rationalization** – Eliminating underperforming product variations to reduce inventory complexity.

📌 **Example: How ITC Reduced Manufacturing Costs by 18%** ITC streamlined its **supply chain and packaging procurement** to lower costs while maintaining product quality, improving net profits by **5% YoY.**

👉 **Lesson: Cost-cutting should be strategic, not blind expense reductions.**

🚀 FINAL TAKEAWAY: PROFITABILITY IN FMCG IS AN ART & SCIENCE

Scaling in FMCG is about **balancing sales growth, pricing, trade promotions, marketing, and operational efficiency.** A company that scales **without profitability insights** will burn through cash, while one that optimizes costs and investments will **build a sustainable business.**

- **Track ROI beyond sales figures.**
- **Pricing strategies should adapt as the brand scales.**
- **Inventory & supply chain efficiency drive profitability.**

- Trade promotions must be high-impact, not random discounts.
- Marketing ROI should be data-driven, not vanity metrics.

With this, we conclude FMCG Blueprint—your no-nonsense guide to FMCG success!

Product rotation refers to **the speed at which inventory cycles through the supply chain.** The faster a product moves, the more frequently it needs restocking. The slower a product moves, the more storage and marketing support it requires.

FMCG PRODUCTS CAN GENERALLY BE CATEGORIZED INTO THREE TYPES

1. Superfast-Moving Products (Daily Essentials)

- **Examples:** Milk, Bread, Eggs, Cigarettes, Soft Drinks
- **Rotation Speed:** Within 24-48 hours
- **Key Challenge:** Constant restocking and minimizing out-of-stock situations

These products are high-frequency purchases, meaning they need to be **available at all times** to maintain customer loyalty. Any delay in restocking results in **immediate lost sales and market share to competitors.**

☑ **Best Practices for Superfast-Moving Products:**

- o Maintain **just-in-time inventory** to prevent overstocking or spoilage.
- o Use **real-time demand forecasting tools** to avoid shortages.
- o Work closely with distributors for **fast replenishment cycles.**

🔹 **Case Study: How Coca-Cola Manages Ultra-Fast Rotation** Coca-Cola operates on a **24-hour replenishment cycle** in key markets, ensuring that their beverages are **always available** at kirana stores and supermarkets. They use advanced **demand prediction algorithms** to stock up just before a peak sales period.

👉 **Lesson:** Fast-moving products require **aggressive distribution and zero stockouts.**

2. Fast-Moving Products (Staples & Everyday Items)

⚡ **Examples:** Biscuits, Chips, Soap, Detergent, Instant Noodles ⚡ **Rotation Speed:** 3-10 days ⚡ **Key Challenge:** Balancing stock levels without overloading inventory

Fast-moving products do not expire as quickly as perishable items, but they still require **frequent restocking and promotional support** to maintain demand.

✅ **Best Practices for Fast-Moving Products:**

- o Use **automated stock replenishment systems** to prevent overstocking.
- o Deploy **dynamic shelf space management**—increase space for high-demand SKUs.
- o Offer **combo packs and promotions** to increase volume sales.

📌 **Example: How Britannia Drives Biscuit Sales** Britannia uses **limited-time offers, festive packs, and bulk promotions** to drive higher biscuit sales during peak demand periods like Diwali. This helps move inventory faster and **creates an urgency among retailers to stock up.**

👉 **Lesson:** Smart promotions can accelerate **medium-speed rotation categories.**

3. Slow-Moving but High-Margin Products (Luxury & Personal Care)

- 🔹 **Examples:** Premium Cosmetics, Perfumes, Specialty Chocolates, High-End Personal Care
- 🔹 **Rotation Speed:** 30-90 days
- 🔹 **Key Challenge:** Preventing stockpiling and minimizing unsold inventory

Slow-moving products tend to have **higher profit margins**, but retailers are reluctant to stock them in large quantities because they take longer to sell.

✅ **Best Practices for Slow-Moving Products:**

- o Offer **exclusive in-store experiences** (sampling stations, tester units).
- o Use **targeted promotions like 'Buy 1 Get 1 Free'** to speed up movement.
- o Adopt **e-commerce strategies**—since these products sell better online due to price sensitivity.

📢 **Example: How L'Oréal Moves Slow-Moving Premium Products** L'Oréal partners with **beauty advisors in modern trade outlets** to promote their premium skincare range. By using **educational marketing**, they convert casual buyers into high-value customers, increasing rotation speed.

👉 **Lesson:** Slow-moving products need **stronger push marketing efforts** to sell effectively.

6.8 - MANAGING INVENTORY FOR DIFFERENT ROTATION CATEGORIES

Managing inventory across different product categories requires **a flexible approach** that adapts to the unique needs of each segment.

1. FIFO VS. LIFO: CHOOSING THE RIGHT INVENTORY MANAGEMENT APPROACH

- o **FIFO (First In, First Out):** Ideal for **superfast-moving and perishable goods** to prevent expiration.
- o **LIFO (Last In, First Out):** Works well for **high-margin, slow-moving goods** where price appreciation plays a role.

Example: How Dairy Brands Manage FIFO Amul ensures that **older stock is sold first** using a **strict FIFO policy** to maintain freshness across its supply chain.

2. HANDLING OVERSTOCK VS. STOCKOUTS

Balancing **supply and demand** is the ultimate goal of FMCG inventory management.

- ☑ **To Avoid Stockouts:** Use **real-time inventory tracking, demand forecasting, and distributor partnerships.**
- ☑ **To Avoid Overstocking:** Implement **sales-driven stock allocation** and use **seasonal demand planning**.

Example: How Nestlé Manages Stock Levels for Maggi Nestlé adjusts **production cycles and distributor allocation** based on demand forecasts, preventing Maggi from going out of stock while avoiding overproduction.

Lesson: Accurate forecasting and smart stock control prevent both lost sales and excessive storage costs.

6.9 - OPTIMIZING PROFITABILITY ACROSS DIFFERENT PRODUCT CATEGORIES

Since different FMCG products rotate at **different speeds**, pricing and promotion strategies must be **adjusted to ensure profitability.**

1. Superfast-Moving Products – Focus on Volume Sales

Low margins, but massive volume sales. **Example:** A local dairy brand makes **thin margins on milk sales but profits through sheer volume.**

2. Fast-Moving Products – Balance Volume & Margin

Example: Biscuits and packaged snacks balance **bulk sales with seasonal promotions to maintain profits.**

3. Slow-Moving, High-Margin Products – Justify the Premium

Example: High-end chocolates charge **premium pricing**, supported by branding and storytelling.

Lesson: Each category requires a different approach to pricing, promotions, and profit optimization.

- Superfast-moving products require perfect stock replenishment and demand forecasting.

- Fast-moving products need sales-boosting promotions and smart shelf space allocation.

- Slow-moving products require brand positioning, storytelling, and premium pricing.

- Inventory management must be customized for each product type.

 **NEXT UP**

The Psychology of FMCG Buying – How Brands Hack Your Brain!

PART 4:
MARKETING, BRANDING & THE BATTLE FOR CONSUMER ATTENTION

CHAPTER 7

THE PSYCHOLOGY OF FMCG BUYING –
HOW BRANDS HACK YOUR BRAIN

Every time you pick up a snack, a shampoo, or a soda, **you think you're making a choice.** In reality, FMCG brands have spent **billions of dollars** studying consumer psychology to ensure you buy **their** product over the competition. From packaging tricks to pricing strategies, let's dive into **how brands manipulate buying decisions** (and how you can use these insights to win in FMCG!).

7.1 – THE CONSUMER BUYING PROCESS – HOW DECISIONS ARE MADE

Unlike durable goods, where consumers **spend weeks researching before making a purchase**, FMCG products are often bought **on impulse.** The decision-making process is **quick, habitual, and influenced by branding, pricing, and placement.**

THE FIVE STAGES OF THE FMCG BUYING JOURNEY (AND WHAT REALLY HAPPENS IN A SHOPPER'S MIND)

1. Problem Recognition – The "Oh No, We're Out!" Moment

This is where it all starts. You open your fridge and realize there's no milk for your morning chai. Or worse, you're halfway through a shower and your shampoo bottle is as empty as your motivation on a Monday morning.

👉 **Brand Trick:** Brands ensure their logos are visible on packaging **even when the product is nearly empty**, subtly reminding consumers to repurchase (ever noticed how the Coca-Cola logo is printed on the inside of their bottle labels?).

2. Information Search – The "What Should I Buy?" Dilemma

In FMCG, consumers don't always do deep research, but they do rely on **past experiences, advertisements, and peer recommendations.**

Example: You need biscuits for your tea. You could go for **Parle-G (nostalgia + affordability), Bourbon (indulgence), or NutriChoice (health guilt).** Your choice is subconsciously influenced by past ads, price, and which brand was most visible in the store.

👉 **Brand Trick:** Supermarkets place big brands at **eye level** while keeping store-brand alternatives on lower shelves. Why? **Because consumers are lazy.**

3. Evaluation of Alternatives – The "Is It Worth It ?" Moment

This is where shoppers do quick mental calculations:

- *Do I stick to my usual brand, or try something new?*
- *Should I buy the large pack to save money or stick with the smaller one?*
- *Is the buy-one-get-one-free offer really a deal, or am I getting scammed?*

👉 **Brand Trick:** Ever noticed why a **250ml shampoo costs ₹99, but a 500ml pack costs ₹175?** That's called **price anchoring**—brands make the bigger pack **seem like a steal** by pricing the smaller one disproportionately high.

4. Purchase Decision – The "Let's Just Buy It" Step

The shopper finally makes a choice, often based on a mix of **habit, price, packaging, and convenience.** But the battle isn't over yet—**checkout counter placements** (like chocolates, gum, and small beauty products) try to **squeeze out one last impulse purchase.**

👉 **Brand Trick:** Retailers use **"limited-time offer" signs** (even when the offer has existed for months) to create **a false sense of urgency.**

5. Post-Purchase Behavior – The "Did I Make the Right Choice?" Feeling

Once home, consumers either:

- **Feel satisfied** (leading to repeat purchases and brand loyalty). ✅
- **Regret their choice** (leading them to switch brands next time). ✖

👉 **Brand Trick:** Ever noticed brands **launch "new and improved" versions frequently?** This reassures customers that they made the right choice, even when the product is **almost identical to the previous version.**

7.2 - THE ROLE OF COGNITIVE BIASES IN FMCG PURCHASES (HOW BRANDS TRICK YOUR BRAIN)

Consumers like to think they make **rational** choices, but in reality, the human brain is lazy. **It relies on mental shortcuts to make decisions quickly**, and FMCG brands **exploit these shortcuts** to drive sales.

1. THE ANCHORING EFFECT – SETTING A PRICE REFERENCE

Your brain **compares new prices against the first price it sees.** This is why brands show **higher "original prices"** before revealing the "discounted price."

👉 **Example:** Big Bazaar advertises *"₹200 OFF on groceries above ₹999"*, making you feel like you're saving money—even if you **weren't planning to buy ₹999 worth of groceries in the first place!**

👉 **Brand Trick:** MRP strikes (₹100 → ₹79) make consumers **believe they're getting a deal, even when the discount is negligible.**

2. THE DECOY EFFECT – STEERING YOU TOWARDS A PREFERRED CHOICE

Brands **intentionally introduce a "bad" option** to make another option look better.

👉 **Example:** A juice brand offers:

- 200ml pack – ₹30
- 500ml pack – ₹80
- 1L pack – ₹85 (only ₹5 more for double the size!)

The **500ml pack exists just to make 1L look like a better deal.**

👉 **Brand Trick:** By placing an unattractive middle option, brands can **manipulate consumer choice.**

3. LOSS AVERSION – FEAR OF MISSING OUT (FOMO)

Consumers **hate losing out more than they enjoy gaining.** Brands use this to create urgency.

👆 **Example:** Amazon shows **"Only 2 left in stock"** to make you buy instantly, even if it restocks the next day.

👆 **Brand Trick:** Flash sales, countdown timers, and "Buy Now or Regret Later" messaging **pressure consumers into impulsive buying.**

4. THE FRAMING EFFECT – HOW WORDING CHANGES PERCEPTION

Consumers interpret the same information differently **depending on how it's presented.**

👆 **Example:** Would you rather buy a yogurt labeled **"90% Fat-Free"** or **"10% Fat"**? Most people choose the first—even though they're identical.

👆 **Brand Trick:** Words like **"Guilt-Free"**, **"Low-Calorie"**, or **"Rich & Creamy"** tap into emotions rather than facts.

(And Why You Always End Up Buying More Than Planned)

How Colors Influence Perception:

- ● **Blue (Trust, Purity):** Used in water brands like Bisleri.

- ● **Red (Excitement, Appetite):** Common in snack foods (Lay's, Coca-Cola).

- ● **Green (Health, Natural):** Often used for organic or 'healthy' products.

📌 **Example:** Ever noticed **why premium brands use minimalistic packaging?** Less clutter = higher perceived quality.

👉 **Lesson:** The **outside of the product** matters as much as what's inside!

Retail Execution – Winning at the Shelf!

CHAPTER 8
RETAIL EXECUTION – WINNING AT THE SHELF

You can have the best product, the most aggressive pricing, and a killer marketing campaign—but if your product isn't **visible, available, and irresistible** at the point of sale, it won't move. **Retail execution is where the real FMCG battle is fought and won.**

8.1 - THE THREE PILLARS OF RETAIL EXECUTION

Winning in retail execution is about **mastering three fundamental aspects:**

1. AVAILABILITY – ENSURING YOUR PRODUCT IS ALWAYS STOCKED

Product availability is the most fundamental aspect of FMCG sales. **If your product isn't available at the store when a customer wants to buy it, the sale is lost, and a competitor wins.**

Challenges in Availability:

- **Stockouts due to poor demand forecasting** – Retailers often under-order or distributors fail to replenish stock in time.
- **Irregular order cycles** – Some retailers delay placing new orders, leading to gaps in availability.
- **Distributor inefficiencies** – Some distributors prioritize higher-margin products, causing delays for certain SKUs.
- **Limited shelf space** – Retailers may allocate more space to brands that offer better margins or promotions.

Best Practices to Ensure Availability:

- ☑ **Use real-time inventory tracking** – Advanced POS systems can help retailers and brands track stock levels accurately.
- ☑ **Implement auto-replenishment systems** – Brands can work with retailers to automate reordering based on sales data.
- ☑ **Set up strict distributor SLAs** – Brands should enforce service level agreements with distributors to ensure timely stock replenishment.
- ☑ **Regular mystery shopping audits** – Conduct random store visits to ensure products are consistently available and stocked as per agreements.
- ☑ **Optimize warehouse locations** – Having regional warehouses ensures faster product replenishment and avoids stockouts.

📌 **Example: How Nestlé Ensures Maggi's Uninterrupted Availability** Nestlé uses **a high-frequency distributor replenishment system** that ensures Maggi is always stocked, even in small kirana stores. Their distributors visit key outlets multiple times a week, reducing stockouts significantly.

👉 **Lesson:** If your product is not on the shelf, it will never reach the consumer's hands.

2. VISIBILITY – WINNING THE SHELF PLACEMENT BATTLE

Shelf space is the **most valuable real estate in a retail store**. Consumers make split-second decisions based on **which products are easiest to see and grab.** A product hidden at the bottom shelf has a **70% lower chance** of getting picked compared to one placed at eye level.

Key Elements of Visibility:

- ☑ **Eye-Level = Buy-Level** – Products placed at **eye level** get significantly higher sales than those on the bottom shelf.
- ☑ **Category Adjacency Matters** – Your product should be placed **next to complementary products** (e.g., chips near soft drinks, shampoo near conditioner).
- ☑ **Branded Racks & POSM Materials** – Use **branded shelves, promotional stands, and eye-catching signage** to draw consumer attention.
- ☑ **End-Cap Displays Drive Impulse Purchases** – Brands should negotiate for premium end-cap display spaces near checkout counters.
- ☑ **Cross-Merchandising Strategies** – Placing related products together (e.g., peanut butter next to bread) increases basket size.

🔹 **Example: How Coca-Cola Secures Prime Shelf Space** Coca-Cola pays **slotting fees to retailers** to ensure its bottles are **always placed at eye level in refrigerated sections**, maximizing impulse purchases.

👉 **Lesson:** If your product is not **visible**, it is **invisible to the consumer.**

3. RETAILER RELATIONSHIPS – THE KEY TO GETTING PREFERRED TREATMENT

Retailers play a critical role in determining **which products they promote and prioritize.** The stronger your relationship with them, the **higher your chances of getting premium shelf space and push support.**

Strategies to Build Strong Retailer Relationships:

- ☑ **Offer attractive trade margins & incentives** – Higher margins encourage retailers to push your product over competitors.

- ☑ **Provide in-store promotions & sales schemes** – Exclusive retailer discounts, free stock schemes, and festive promotions help increase sales.

- ☑ **Give training & product education** – Educate retailers about product USPs so they can confidently recommend them to customers.

- ☑ **Ensure hassle-free returns & replacements** – A smooth return policy increases retailer confidence in stocking your brand.

- ☑ **Establish loyalty programs for retailers** – Incentivize long-term stocking and sales push with reward points or bonus margins.

✦ **Example: How ITC's Aashirvaad Atta Built Retailer Loyalty** ITC offers **higher retailer margins, festival-specific bonuses, and exclusive stock incentives,** ensuring Aashirvaad Atta gets **priority placement over competitors like Pillsbury and Annapurna.**

☞ **Lesson:** Retailers **push the products that are most beneficial for them.** Build trust, and they'll help sell your brand.

1. MYSTERY SHOPPING & SHELF MANAGEMENT HANDLING – THE SECRET AUDITS THAT KEEP EXECUTION ON POINT

Mystery shopping is a **covert audit** conducted by brands to evaluate their in-store execution.

- ☑ **Check stock availability** – Ensure products are actually on the shelves, not sitting in storage.
- ☑ **Monitor planogram compliance** – Ensure shelves are arranged as per brand guidelines.
- ☑ **Test retailer product knowledge** – Identify if retailers are pushing competitor brands instead.

◆ **Example: How Unilever Uses Mystery Shopping to Maintain Execution** Unilever regularly sends secret shoppers to **check if Surf Excel's shelf share is maintained** as per agreements with retailers.

2. MERCHANDISING HACKS THAT DRIVE SALES WITHOUT ADVERTISING

Strategic in-store merchandising can increase sales **without additional ad spending.**

- ☑ **Use larger pack sizes to occupy more space.**
- ☑ **Ensure front-facing shelf placement for brand recall.**
- ☑ **Use shelf talkers to highlight key benefits.**

◆ **Example: How Nestlé Boosts Nescafé Sales Through Merchandising** Nestlé uses **prominent shelf branding** and **interactive digital screens** in modern trade outlets to create engagement.

3. TRADE PROMOTIONS: WHAT ACTUALLY WORKS (AND WHAT'S A WASTE OF MONEY)

Not all trade promotions lead to higher sales. Some strategies work better than others.

- ☑ **BOGO (Buy One, Get One Free)** – Effective for increasing trial purchases.
- ☑ **Temporary price reductions** – Best for driving volume but can hurt margins.
- ☑ **Retailer incentives** – More effective than deep consumer discounts.

📌 **Example: How a Brand Increased Sales by 20% Just by Moving Shelves** A juice brand repositioned its product **next to premium water bottles instead of soft drinks**, leading to a **20% sales jump** due to perceived health benefits.

 **NEXT UP**

Scaling an FMCG Brand – From Local Player to Big League!

PART 5:
GROWTH, TRENDS & THRIVING IN FMCG

CHAPTER 9

SCALING AN FMCG BRAND – FROM LOCAL PLAYER TO BIG LEAGUE

So you've built a great product, nailed retail execution, and are generating sales. But how do you scale? **Going from a small regional player to a national or even global FMCG brand isn't just about selling more—it's about scaling smart.**

Distribution is **the lifeblood of FMCG scaling**. A brand cannot grow if it fails to reach new customers in newer geographies. **The key to expansion is building a robust, scalable distribution network that minimizes costs and maximizes reach.**

Key Distribution Strategies for Scaling:

✅ **From Direct to Multi-Level Distribution:** When starting, many brands rely on a **direct distribution model**, serving retailers themselves. However, as a brand grows, it must transition to a **multi-tier distribution system** involving **super-stockists, distributors, and sub-distributors** to ensure deep market penetration.

✅ **Route-to-Market (RTM) Optimization:** Brands must refine their **RTM strategy** based on the target geography. Rural markets require **wholesaler-led distribution**, while urban markets thrive on **modern trade and e-commerce integration. A hybrid model** combining multiple RTM approaches ensures efficiency.

✅ **Leveraging E-Commerce for Scale:** Online grocery platforms like **Amazon, Flipkart, Blinkit, and Zepto** are powerful expansion tools. Small brands can bypass traditional retail barriers and **directly reach end consumers**, gaining nationwide visibility without the heavy investments required for general trade.

📌 **Example: How Paper Boat Expanded Nationally** Paper Boat started as a niche ethnic beverage brand in metro cities, using **direct distribution in key markets**. It later partnered with major distributors and expanded into **modern trade and e-commerce**, scaling across India in just a few years.

👉 **Lesson:** A well-structured distribution strategy **creates the foundation for national expansion.**

Scaling up means handling **higher production volumes, wider distribution networks, and complex inventory management.** Brands must ensure their supply chain **keeps pace with their expansion plans.**

Key Considerations for a Scalable Supply Chain:

☑ **Demand Forecasting & Inventory Planning:** Rapid growth means **increased demand volatility.** Brands must use **predictive analytics and AI-driven forecasting tools** to avoid stockouts and overproduction, keeping supply aligned with demand.

☑ **Regional Warehousing for Faster Replenishment:** As brands scale, they must **move beyond a centralized warehouse** and establish **multiple regional fulfillment centers** to reduce lead times and logistics costs. **A distributed warehousing model** improves efficiency and ensures faster delivery to retailers.

☑ **Optimizing Manufacturing Costs:** Mass production can **lower per-unit costs,** but brands must **balance economies of scale with operational efficiency.** Leveraging **third-party manufacturers (contract manufacturing)** can help brands expand production **without heavy CapEx investments.**

📌 **Example: How Patanjali Managed Hypergrowth** Patanjali rapidly expanded its product portfolio and distribution in just a few years. To manage demand, it **outsourced production** to third-party manufacturers while setting up its own plants for core products, ensuring a **cost-effective and flexible supply chain.**

👉 **Lesson: A supply chain built for scale ensures consistent product availability while keeping costs in check.**

9.3 - MARKETING & BRAND BUILDING – CREATING A NATIONAL IDENTITY

Scaling isn't just about selling more—it's about building a **strong brand identity that resonates across diverse consumer segments.** A brand that works in **one region** may not connect the same way in another.

How to Build a Scalable Brand Identity:

✅ **Maintaining Core Brand Values While Adapting Locally:** Brands must balance **consistency and localization**—a product like Maggi retains its global identity while offering **regional flavors** to cater to local tastes.

✅ **Multi-Channel Marketing Approach:** A national brand needs to engage consumers across **TV, digital, print, and in-store promotions.** The **media mix should evolve** based on market maturity—smaller brands focus on digital first, while larger brands expand into mass media.

✅ **Influencer & Community Marketing:** Scaling brands must build trust **at a grassroots level.** Collaborations with **regional influencers, micro-influencers, and local events** help **deepen consumer connections** beyond traditional advertising.

🔸 **Example: How Amul Became a Household Name** Amul scaled not just through distribution but through **consistent branding, humorous advertising, and regional product innovation.** Their iconic **Amul girl campaigns** helped build **mass recall across multiple generations.**

👉 **Lesson: Marketing must evolve as the brand scales—what works for a small brand may not work for a national player.**

Pricing plays a **critical role in expansion**. A brand's **pricing strategy at launch may not be sustainable at scale**—it needs to be optimized for **cost efficiency, market competition, and profitability.**

Pricing Strategies for Scale:

- ✅ **Balancing Price & Volume:** Small brands often use **penetration pricing** to attract early customers. As they scale, they must gradually **increase margins** without alienating consumers.

- ✅ **Regional Pricing Adjustments:** Price sensitivity varies across markets. Brands must adopt **region-specific pricing models**, offering **smaller, lower-cost SKUs for rural markets** while keeping **premium SKUs for urban consumers.**

- ✅ **Bundling & Upselling Strategies:** Larger brands use **combo packs, family packs, and value bundles** to increase overall ticket size while keeping per-unit prices competitive.

📌 **Example: How HUL Adjusted Pricing for Growth** HUL's **Lifebuoy and Clinic Plus** shampoos started with small **sachet pricing** to penetrate rural markets. Once demand scaled, **larger packs with higher margins** were introduced to **maximize profitability.**

👉 **Lesson: Pricing should evolve as the brand scales—what works for initial growth may not be sustainable long-term.**

For brands aiming for global expansion, **international markets come with their own complexities.** Brands must adapt to **new regulations, consumer preferences, and distribution challenges.**

Key Strategies for International Expansion:

- ✅ **Understanding Market Entry Barriers:** Regulatory approvals, labeling laws, and import duties **must be navigated carefully** when entering foreign markets.

- ✅ **Partnering with Local Distributors:** Instead of setting up infrastructure immediately, brands can **work with local distributors or retail chains** to test-market their products.

- ✅ **Product Adaptation & Localization:** What works in one country **may not work elsewhere.** Brands like **KFC & McDonald's** tweak menus to match local food habits, and FMCG brands must do the same.

🔖 **Example: How Dabur Expanded Internationally** Dabur successfully expanded into the Middle East and North Africa by **adapting its Ayurveda-based offerings** to local consumer preferences and **partnering with regional distributors** for market entry.

👉 **Lesson: Global scaling requires local adaptation—brands that ignore this fail.**

The Future of FMCG – Where the Industry is Headed!

CHAPTER 10
THE FUTURE OF FMCG – WHERE THE INDUSTRY IS HEADED

The FMCG industry is evolving faster than ever, shaped by **changing consumer behavior, technological advancements, and sustainability demands.** Brands that adapt will thrive; those that don't will fade into history. So, where is FMCG headed in the next decade? Let's break it down.

E-commerce is no longer just a **channel**—for many FMCG brands, it's becoming the **primary sales engine**. Traditional retail models are being disrupted as consumers shift to **online grocery platforms, quick commerce, and direct brand engagement.**

Key Drivers of E-Commerce FMCG Growth:

☑ **Quick Commerce & On-Demand Delivery:** Platforms like **Blinkit, Zepto, and Instamart** are redefining convenience by delivering groceries in **10-30 minutes**. Brands must optimize their supply chains for faster fulfillment.

☑ **Direct-to-Consumer (D2C) Boom:** FMCG giants are cutting out middlemen and selling **directly via their websites and social media. Brands like Mamaearth & The Whole Truth Foods** have scaled entirely through **D2C-first strategies.**

☑ **AI-Driven Personalized Shopping:** Platforms use **AI-powered recommendations** to offer personalized product suggestions based on past purchases, **increasing basket size.**

📌 **Example: How HUL is Leading the Digital Shift** HUL launched **Shikhar, a B2B ordering platform,** allowing retailers to buy directly from them. This **eliminates dependency on traditional distributors** and creates **a direct sales ecosystem.**

👉 **Lesson: FMCG brands must rethink their retail strategy and shift toward an e-commerce-first mindset.**

As FMCG brands scale, **AI, machine learning, and automation** are transforming **supply chains, inventory management, and demand forecasting.** These technologies **reduce costs, improve efficiency, and enhance agility.**

How AI & Automation Are Reshaping FMCG:

- ☑ **Predictive Demand Forecasting:** AI can **analyze sales trends** and **predict stock requirements**, preventing **overstocking and stockouts.**

- ☑ **Automated Warehouses & Smart Logistics:** Robotics and AI-driven **automated warehouses** are speeding up **order fulfillment** while reducing labor costs.

- ☑ **AI-Powered Pricing & Promotions:** AI-driven algorithms help brands set **dynamic pricing based on demand, seasonality, and competitor behavior.**

📌 **Example: Coca-Cola's AI-Powered Demand Forecasting** Coca-Cola uses **real-time analytics** to optimize **distribution routes and retailer stock levels,** ensuring minimal stockouts and reducing wastage.

👉 **Lesson: The brands that adopt AI and automation will dominate the future of FMCG.**

10.3 - SUSTAINABILITY & ETHICAL FMCG – THE GREEN REVOLUTION

Consumers are increasingly demanding **sustainable, ethically sourced, and environmentally friendly** products. The **future of FMCG belongs to brands that prioritize sustainability.**

Key Sustainability Trends Shaping FMCG:

✅ **Plastic-Free & Eco-Friendly Packaging:** Brands are shifting to **biodegradable, recyclable, and refillable packaging** to reduce waste.

✅ **Carbon-Neutral Manufacturing:** FMCG companies are investing in **solar-powered factories and energy-efficient production** to cut carbon footprints.

✅ **Ethical Sourcing & Transparency:** Consumers want to know **where their products come from**—brands that provide supply chain transparency **build stronger trust.**

📌 **Example: Unilever's Sustainable Living Plan** Unilever is on track to make **100% of its plastic packaging recyclable, reusable, or compostable by 2025** while ensuring all ingredients are **sustainably sourced.**

👉 **Lesson: Sustainability is no longer an option—it's a necessity for long-term growth.**

10.4 -PERSONALIZATION & HYPERLOCALIZATION – THE FUTURE OF CONSUMER ENGAGEMENT

Modern consumers expect **products and experiences tailored to their preferences**. Brands that **customize offerings based on region, taste, and buying behavior** will stand out.

Key Personalization Trends in FMCG:

- ✅ **AI-Powered Product Recommendations:** AI enables brands to **predict individual consumer preferences** and suggest personalized products.

- ✅ **Region-Specific Product Variants:** Brands are launching **hyperlocal flavors and formats** to cater to diverse consumer preferences (e.g., Maggi's **regional masala variants** in India).

- ✅ **Interactive Shopping Experiences:** FMCG brands are using **augmented reality (AR)** and gamified experiences to engage consumers online.

➤ **Example: Nestlé's Personalized Nutrition Initiative** Nestlé has invested in **personalized health & wellness brands,** allowing consumers to receive **AI-driven diet plans and customized nutritional products.**

👉 **Lesson: Personalization is the future of FMCG marketing. Consumers don't just want products—they want experiences.**

10.5 - THE EVOLUTION OF RETAIL – FROM MODERN TRADE TO SMART STORES

Physical retail isn't dying—it's evolving. **Smart stores, cashier-less checkouts, and AI-powered retail analytics** are changing how consumers shop.

How Retail is Evolving:

✅ **Cashier-Less & Smart Stores:** AI-driven retail formats like **Amazon Go** eliminate checkout queues with **automated billing systems.**

✅ **Self-Service Kiosks & Digital Shopping Assistants:** Smart kiosks enable **faster, data-driven shopping experiences** inside supermarkets.

✅ **Retailer-Brand Collaborations:** FMCG brands are working directly with modern retailers for **exclusive product launches & private label collaborations.**

📌 **Example: Amazon's Just Walk Out Technology** Amazon Go stores use **AI-powered sensors to track purchases** and bill customers automatically—removing the need for checkout counters.

👉 **Lesson: Retail is no longer about transactions—it's about seamless, tech-driven experiences.**

FMCG'S FUTURE IS TECH-DRIVEN, SUSTAINABLE & CONSUMER-CENTRIC

The future of FMCG belongs to **brands that innovate, embrace technology, and focus on sustainability.** Companies that fail to adapt will become obsolete, while those that **anticipate trends and evolve** will dominate.

- **E-commerce and quick commerce will redefine distribution.**
- **AI and automation will make supply chains smarter.**
- **Sustainability will be a must-have, not a choice.**
- **Personalization will drive consumer engagement.**
- **Smart retail will reshape in-store shopping.**

📖 **With this, we conclude FMCG Blueprint—your no-nonsense guide to FMCG success!** 🎉

CRACKING AN FMCG SALES JOB LIKE A PRO 🚀

Breaking into the **FMCG industry** isn't just about having a degree - it's about knowing the **unwritten rules** of hiring, negotiating the best salary, and picking the right **career path** that actually leads to leadership roles. This chapter will give you an **insider's roadmap** to landing, growing, and thriving in an **FMCG sales career** like a pro.

Unlike traditional industries, FMCG companies look for a **specific kind of candidate**. While a strong CV helps, recruiters focus on **practical sales skills, adaptability, and real-world execution ability.**

What recruiters won't tell you but expect from every candidate:

- ☑ **You need to be field-ready.** Sales jobs in FMCG are **not desk jobs**—be ready to **hit the market daily**, talk to distributors, and **close deals under pressure.**

- ☑ **Your college name matters, but your hustle matters more.** Top companies (P&G, Nestlé, Unilever) prefer **Tier-1 B-schools**, but anyone can break in with the right **sales acumen** and network.

- ☑ **Soft skills matter as much as sales numbers.** Your ability to **influence** retailers, **negotiate margins**, and **handle objections smoothly** is often more important than your technical knowledge.

- ☑ **Data skills are now a must.** With **e-commerce and modern trade booming,** knowing how to use **sales dashboards, CRM tools, and Excel analytics** will give you an edge.

How to stand out in a sea of applicants:

- ◆ **Crack the "Why FMCG Sales?" question.** Employers want people who understand that **sales is the heart of FMCG**—not just a stepping stone.

- ◆ **Be prepared for market-based questions.** Expect scenarios like: *"A distributor refuses to stock your product due to low margins. What will you do?"*

- ◆ **Have a killer elevator pitch.** Most recruiters won't read your entire CV. Instead, **summarize your skills in 30 seconds** focusing on **past sales achievements, negotiation experience, and leadership potential.**

 Pro Tip: If you don't get into a top FMCG brand immediately, **start with a distributor role, GT sales, or modern trade sales in a smaller brand**—then lateral shift after **1-2 years.**

2 - HOW TO NEGOTIATE BETTER PAY (WITHOUT SOUNDING GREEDY) 💰

FMCG brands are known for **structured salary bands**, but **top candidates always negotiate better.** Here's how:

☑️ **Know the industry benchmarks.** ASM (Area Sales Manager) roles typically pay between **₹8-20 LPA**, depending on the company and experience.

☑️ **Don't just negotiate salary—focus on bonuses & benefits.** Many FMCG companies offer **quarterly sales incentives, stock options, car allowances, and relocation benefits**—these can add up to **30% more earnings.**

☑️ **Leverage multiple offers.** The easiest way to negotiate higher is to have another **competing offer** in hand—HR will **always** match or improve their offer if you're a strong candidate.

Real-world script to negotiate like a pro:

🚀 *"I'm really excited about this opportunity and the impact I can create in FMCG sales. Given my experience in [sales execution/distribution/channel management], and the industry benchmarks, I was expecting a package closer to ₹XX LPA. Is there flexibility in the bonus structure or allowances?"*

What happens next? HR will usually **increase bonuses, offer a better allowance, or provide a joining incentive** instead of just increasing the fixed salary. That's still a **win for you!**

3 - THE BEST CAREER PATHS (FROM AREA SALES MANAGER TO CEO) 

Most FMCG leaders started in **sales**. Here's a typical career roadmap:

Step 1: Area Sales Manager (ASM)

- **Your job:** Managing distributors, achieving sales targets, and pushing execution at the ground level.
- **Skills required:** Retail execution, negotiation, distributor handling.
- **Timeline:** 1-3 years before promotion.

Step 2: Regional Sales Manager (RSM)

- **Your job:** Overseeing multiple ASMs across a region, driving revenue, and handling channel conflicts.
- **Skills required:** People management, RTM strategy, pricing & margins.
- **Timeline:** 3-5 years before moving up.

Step 3: National Sales Manager / Trade Marketing Head

- Your job: Driving national-level growth, handling modern trade, e-commerce, and general trade strategies.
- Skills required: Large-scale sales planning, GTM strategy, stakeholder management.
- Timeline: 5-7 years before moving up.

Step 4: Sales Director / VP of Sales

- **Your job:** Overseeing the entire **sales and distribution** network of an FMCG giant.
- **Skills required:** Leadership, P&L responsibility, deep industry insights.

💡 **Pro Tip:** If you want to become **CEO in FMCG**, focus on **P&L experience** and **cross-functional roles in marketing & operations** after 8-10 years in sales.

- **Be data-driven.** Modern FMCG sales require **strong analytics—** tracking sales trends, stock rotations, and trade margins will set you apart.

- **Master distributor handling.** Your success in the early years **depends entirely on retailer and distributor relationships.** Learn how to **incentivize them** without cutting into margins.

- **Don't ignore modern trade & e-commerce.** While GT (General Trade) still rules, **FMCG brands are shifting towards Amazon, Flipkart, and D2C models.** Learn the **pricing and execution strategies** for these channels early.

- **Network like crazy.** Most sales promotions happen due to **internal referrals.** Stay connected to **mentors, peers, and industry leaders.**

🚀 FINAL TAKEAWAY

Breaking into FMCG sales is about **smart positioning, networking, and real execution skills**. The industry rewards **grit, speed, and adaptability**—if you master those, you'll rise **faster than your competition!**